Measurement
Action

by Lindsay Benjamin

Consultant: Brad Laager, MA, Math Educator
Little Falls Community Middle School

for early readers

QC
92.5
.B46
2006

Yellow Umbrella Books are published by Red Brick Learning
7825 Telegraph Road, Bloomington, Minnesota 55438
http://www.redbricklearning.com

Editorial Director: Mary Lindeen
Senior Editor: Hollie J. Endres
Senior Designer: Gene Bentdahl
Photo Researcher: Signature Design
Developer: Raindrop Publishing
Consultant: Brad Laager, MA, Math Educator, Little Falls Community Middle School
Conversion Assistants: Jenny Marks, Laura Manthe

Library of Congress Cataloging-in-Publication Data
Benjamin, Lindsay
   Measurement Action! / by Lindsay Benjamin.
      p. cm.
   ISBN 0-7368-5856-3 (hardcover)
   ISBN 0-7368-5286-7 (softcover)
   1. Weights and measures—Juvenile literature. 2. Metric system—Juvenile literature. I. Title.
   QC92.5.B46 2005
   530.8'1—dc22
                                                        2005015714

Photo Credits:
Cover: PhotoDisc Images; Title Page: Jupiter Images; Page 2: Signature Design; Page 3: Tom
Stewart/Corbis; Page 4: Blend Images; Page 5: Philip James Corwin/Corbis; Page 6: Signature
Design; Page 7: Oliver Multhaup/EPA Photos; Page 8: Phil Greer/KRT; Page 9: Dennis
Curran/Index Stock Imagery; Page 10: Lannis Waters; Palm Beach Post/ZUMA Press; Page 11:
Richard Sobol/ZUMA Press; Page 12: Jupiter Images; Page 13: Comstock Photos; Page 14:
Signature Design

1 2 3 4 5 6 11 10 09 08 07 06

Table of Contents

Standard or Metric?

You can measure things using the size of your foot or hand, but that would just be a guess. To be more exact, we need units of measure that will always be the same.

We use **Standard** and **Metric** measures to find the length, width, and weight of things. Let's find out what Standard and Metric measurement are all about!

How Long? How Wide?

12 inches = 1 foot

When we measure the **length** and **width** of a rug, or a friend's height, for example, we measure in *feet*. To measure something smaller we use *inches*. These are Standard measurements.

You can also measure small things using *centimeters*. Centimeters are smaller than inches. Centimeters are a Metric measurement.

3   feet   = 1 yard
36 inches = 1 yard

In Standard measurement, we use *yards* to tell us how long or how wide large things are. Your teacher's arm is probably almost as long as a yard. We measure things like rooms, fabric, and rope in yards.

A *meter* is the Metric way to tell the length and width of larger things. A meter is a little longer than a yard. Olympic-sized pools are measured in meters.

100 centimeters = 1 meter

How Far?

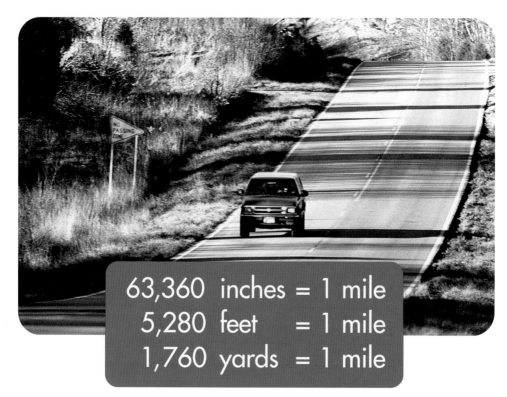

63,360 inches	=	1 mile
5,280 feet	=	1 mile
1,760 yards	=	1 mile

We can travel in many ways. We can take a long walk, travel by car or bicycle, or on a train or airplane. You can measure how far you travel. The Standard system measures long **distances** in *miles*.

The Metric system measures long distances in *kilometers*. A kilometer is as long as a thousand meters.

100,000	centimeters	= 1 kilometer
1,000	meters	= 1 kilometer

How Heavy?
How Light?

16 ounces   = 1 pound
2,000 pounds = 1 ton

To find the **weight** of very light things like a bird, use *ounces*. To measure your weight, use *pounds*. The weight of an elephant can be measured in *tons*!

In the Metric system, *grams* are used to weigh light things. One gram weighs less than one ounce. A *kilogram* measures the weight of heavier things. A kilogram weighs a little more than 2 pounds. The weight of an elephant is measured in *Metric tons.*

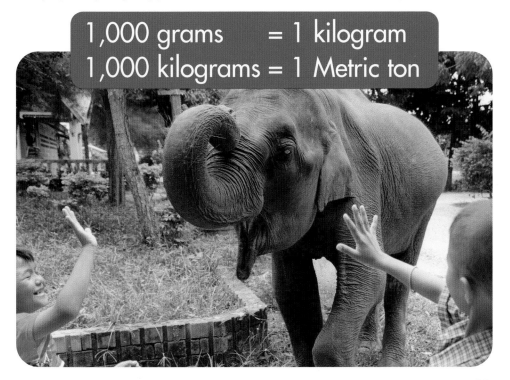

1,000 grams   = 1 kilogram
1,000 kilograms = 1 Metric ton

11

How Hot?
How Cold?

Freezing = 32 degrees Fahrenheit

Temperature is measured in degrees. The colder it is, the lower the number. On the Fahrenheit scale, which is the Standard measurement, water freezes at 32 degrees. That's very cold!

The Metric system also uses degrees to measure temperature. But the Metric measurement is different from the Standard measurement. Water freezes at 0 degrees Celsius, which is the Metric temperature scale.

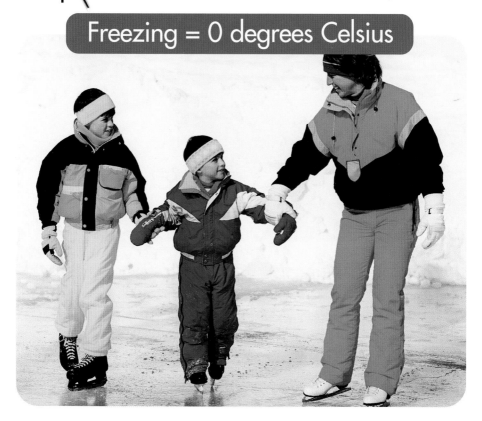

Freezing = 0 degrees Celsius

Time to Measure!

Imagine that you wanted to know this dog's weight. Would miles or kilometers tell you? Pounds or kilograms? Yards or meters?

There's a world of things to measure. Find out length, weight, distance, or how hot or cold something is. It's fun to measure! Try it and see!

Glossary

distance—the space between two places

length—the measurement of the long side of an object

Metric—a system of measurement based on tens

Standard—a system of measurement used only in the United States

temperaure—the measure of how hot or cold something is

weight—the measure of how heavy an object is

width—the measure of the short side of an object

Index

Word Count: 415
Early-Intervention Level: K